Praise for R. Nik Macioci:

"How do you make sense of a life? R. Nicholas Macioci does not provide any answers, nor should he. Rather, he posits life as a series of encounters in bars, chance meetings, dinner dates, and missed connections. Even though he states he's "had enough of memory. That is all / there is," and he's resolved "not to look at all," he is unflinching. His work is about capturing, about the hard stare at yourself in the mirror behind the bar. And like that look at yourself, this collection is full of bright lights, twinkling sounds on a dark guitar."

-Nadia Arioli, author of *Juice*

"Truly, if poetry begins with an observant eye, then we have found our perennial scout. In *Dark Guitar*, truth is spotted at the back of the bar, in church signs and even plates of pasta, and of course in mirrors eager to pin the blame on their admirers. This keen eye is accompanied by a soulful, sage voice. After reading Macioci, your bones grow stronger and wiser -- wearing his experiences as your own, finding cause to look a little closer at your surroundings. "

-Timothy Tarkelly, author of *Luckhound* and
Gently in Manner, Strongly in Deed: Poems on Eisenhower

More praise for R. Nik Macioci:

"The two epigraphs at the beginning of this book of poems by R. Nikolas Macioci, hint at a diverse, musical, and emotional collection of powerful poems. The quotes from B. B. King and Andres Segovia prepare the reader for lines like, 'slipped a knife into me or punched/until blood gleamed in the moonlight' ("A Short-lived Spree") or 'By morning I will have forgotten/that I even said these things,/that I pleaded with myself not to scream/into the night for a knock at the door' ("April 27, 2019 Evening Wish"). Mr. Macioci's 158 pages of strong, honest poems will take the reader on a beautiful ride through a landscape that is frightening and pure – in a Frank O'Hara way!! Read and swallow each poem until the last lines of this book of raving intimacies: 'I am the expert, the kid who once hid/in the closet because, at the time,/it seemed the safest place to be' ("Hidden Guitar")."

-Michael Poage, author, *You Must Have Your Famine,* michaelpoage.com

DARK GUITAR

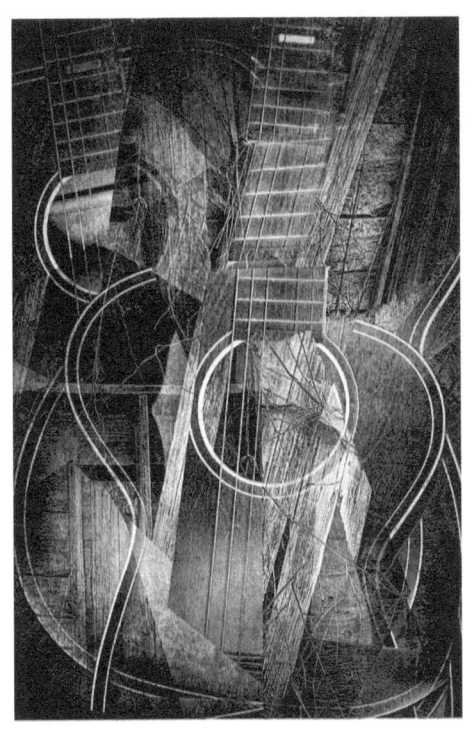

Poems by R. Nikolas Macioci

Kung Fu Treachery Press
Rancho Cucamonga, CA

Copyright © R. Nikolas Macioci
First Edition: 1 3 5 7 9 10 8 6 4 2
ISBN: 978-1-952411-44-1
LCCN: 2021930793

Cover art: Georges Braque, courtesy of the Museum of Modern Art
Author photo: Sandra Feen
All rights reserved. No part of this publication may be
reproduced or transmitted in any form or by any means,
electronic or mechanical, including photocopying,
recording or by info retrieval system, without prior
written permission from the author.

Acknowledgments:

Grateful acknowledgment is made to the following
publications in which some of these poems
first appeared: "Dinner," *The Bombay Review*
"In the Garden of Narcissus," *West Trade Review*
"Dark Guitar" *Ginosko Literary Journal*
"Be Drunk" *Ginosko Literary Journal*
"Jack Daniel's Debut" *Ginosko Literary Journal*
"Bad Words" *Ginosko Literary Journal*
"A Crooked Childhood" *The RavensPerch*
"Jesse Wants to Help You" *The RavensPerch*
"Triggered By a Drink or Two" *The Main Street Rag*
"Who Would Have Known" *Glass Mountain*

TABLE OF CONTENTS

STRUMMING

Dark Guitar / 1

AT THE HOLY BIRD BAR

An Ambivalent Hour / 5

Triggered by a Drink or Two / 7

A Short-Lived Spree / 8

Jack Daniel's Debut / 10

Epistemological Drunk / 12

Savagery / 13

Be Drunk / 15

Wretched Blues and Forlorness of Friday Night / 16

Tonight / 18

To Go Among the Ruins / 20

Cathartic Ceremony / 22

Jesus, Give Me a Jack and Coke / 23

In the Garden of Narcissus / 24

Sitting in a Bar for Hours on a Friday Night / 25

Body Truth / 26

The Drag Queen's Bingo Game / 28

Thanksgiving Evening / 30

Empty Town / 32

New Year's Eve, 2018 / 34

I Do Not Sing When I Drink / 36

Force of Heart / 38

Be Careful, Leo / 40
Failed Promises of the Flesh / 42
Friday Night Gathering of Fellows at a Favorite
   Watering Hole / 44
Stripper / 48
A Wrong End to the Night / 48

GOD TRICKS

Which God? / 53
Understanding Such Things as God / 55
God Never Kissed Bobby Wakefield / 56
Johnny Gordon Lets Go With God / 58
Iconoclast / 60
On a Country Road I learned There Is No God / 61
At Woodruff and High / 63
Do Angels Make Love? / 65
Jesse Wants to Help You / 67
Alley Animals / 69
Bad Words / 71
Metaphysics of the Sky / 73
Holy / 75
Stoning Theology / 76

MOMENTARY OCCURRENCES

The Mexicans / 81
After I Got My New Roof / 83
April 27, 2019, Evening Wish / 85
The Shape of Anonymity / 86

You Surprise Me with Your Interest / 87

Paper and Ink / 88

One-Sided / 89

At Flyers Pizza and Sub Shop / 90

Chef / 91

Anatomy of a Momentary Passion / 93

Asian / 95

Benjamin / 97

In the Bank Line / 99

Everything About a Newcomer / 101

TEMPORARY AFFECTIONS

Checking Myself Out / 105

A Thing Predicted / 107

This Sunday / 108

Dinner / 110

Sunglasses / 112

Juan / 114

Tony / 116

You Come My Way, and I Think You're Wicked / 118

You Should Have Come to Me / 120

Explaining Your Body / 122

Exceptional Breakfast / 123

Late Date / 124

Sudden Destiny / 126

H.C. / 128

A Page of Passion from the Book of Blue / 129

IN A LAND OF STONES

Depicting the Sorrow of Being a Childhood Queer / 133

Straightening Up / 135

A Crooked Childhood / 137

The Mingling of Blood / 139

Union Station Is Real / 141

Who Would Have Known? / 143

Self Portrait / 145

Solemnly Alone in the Street / 147

Library Thief / 149

Nowhere Was I More Lonely Than
   at the Pride Parade / 151

Boxes / 153

A MISCELLANEOUS RIFF

Hidden Guitar / 157

For Henry Coleman,
steadfast friend who is always there.

I

STRUMMING

I wanted to connect my guitar to human emotions.

-B.B. King

Lean your body forward slightly to support the guitar against your chest, for the poetry of the music should resound in your heart.

-Andres Segovia

DARK GUITAR

I've always wanted to play guitar
in the dark, a glass of Merlot on
a nearby table. I would walk fingers
toward wine, their tips feeling
for the base. I would lift the glass
to my lips like a surprise kiss that
makes me wonder if I really was alone.
I would close my eyes, strum strings
with one hand and fret with the other.
I would sing "Screaming Infidelities"
while everyone sleeps-- a one-man party
without paper hats and confetti.
I would play and sing until empty
of everything but music. I would stop
when an orange glow of sunrise burns
beyond the window. The wine glass
would fill with light. I would fall asleep,
the guitar slump into my lap.
I would dream about love and how
a single man sings late at night
without candles, without romance.

II

AT THE HOLY BIRD BAR

*Sometimes what I wouldn't give
to have us sitting in a bar again at
9:a.m. Telling lies to one
another, far from God.*

-Denis Johnson, Jesus' Son

*The world is a bar, we all fill
our glasses the way we can.*

-M.F. Moonzajer

AN AMBIVALENT HOUR

I have an hour to kill before my haircut.
I could sit in the parking lot, listen
to rain play a tune on the roof of my car
or stop at the neighborhood saloon
for an early drink. As I pass the bar,
I notice only two cars in the lot which means,
unless I want to talk to the bartender,
there won't be much company to choose from.
I drive on by.

I should have stayed home the extra hour,
but I've been snowed in four days.
Rain has liberated me.

I'm not really a bar boy, didn't inherit alcoholism.
I know a bar is not a place to go for first class
conversation, but I'm of an age when even a stranger's
words matter. You'd have to hold me, however,
at gunpoint to talk about sports, nor am I much
interested in hearing woes of failed marriages.
Mostly, I'm silent, stare into the mirror over the bar,
wish I were younger.

I turn into the hair salon and park.
It has rained enough to require a rowboat.
I still have a little time to kill, so I settle
in my seat and wait. The bar is just down

the street behind me. Maybe I should go back.
Maybe someone would punch me in the arm,
say they haven't seen me for a while. but
I'm not going back because I want to talk
about love and poetry, how I have been drunk
on both without ever having had a drink.
Barflies' brains would bulge disbelief
if I broached such topics. There's a pause
in the rain. I scramble to shelter, desperate
for the right language.

TRIGGERED BY A DRINK OR TWO

It's not easy to be in a bar by myself thinking
about all the James Baldwin books I read
in the sixties. Times change, but not the need
for certain words like "queer" to signify
possibility of love between two men. Back then,
I read page after page, hoping I would come
across something about my own life.

Fifty years later, I'm sitting in this bar
as alone as I was when I read Baldwin's books.
It took decades of failed relationships to learn
what it means to be permanently lonely.

Tonight, I'm drinking Seagram's 7, trying
to get a kick-start for even caring to be alive.
Baby, I would say to the man sitting next to me,
do you think I'm a tramp to come here and drink
until I'm thoroughly buzzed? My life is full
of hidden secrets I don't care to share, secrets
only a heavy drinker can handle. I could tell
you more, but the bartender is wanting to close,
and would have wanted to take me home
sixty years ago.

I settle my bill, and he continues to wipe down
the bar. My definition of reality comes from the bottle.
I'm stuck with the underbelly of identity. Baldwin
was right: It's never easy to be sad, and life is
a place from which to be carried away in arms
that only come in random dreams.

A SHORT-LIVED SPREE

Why would I ever sit in a bar
when my parents dragged me from one
to another when I was growing up?

A few months ago, however, I went
on a spree, frequented one particular bar
several times a week. I don't drink, but
to fit in, I forced myself to sip Jack and Coke.
I would sit and stare at a Bud Light neon sign
until oblivion set in. It was not oblivion
from having drunk too much. It was oblivion
from slipping from self into a vacuum.
I wanted to meet someone who would
say something that mattered. Several times,
I leaned to either side only to be repelled
by uninteresting conversation.

Time after time, I heard screams in my head,
screams of desperation to be connected.

It was not a very satisfying few weeks at the bar.
I burnt away hope as quickly as a smoker burns
away a cigarette, butts of both aimed at the gutter.

I'm lucky not to have been roughed up
coming and going to and from my car.
Bullies could have sneaked from the dark,

slipped a knife into me or punched
until blood gleamed in the moonlight.
I was lucky to be no more than panhandled.

I stopped going to the bar. It was a godawful
waste, a haven for everybody who can't do anything
with their lives but sit on a stool,
wonder where is the person who will love me?

JACK DANIEL'S DEBUT

I recently went into a liquor store
for the first time to purchase a bottle
of Jack Daniel's for medicinal purposes.
Mom always kept whiskey on hand,
made hot toddies to remedy a cold.

I looked around at the other customers
and saw everything from a dapper aristocrat
to a down-and-out derelict. Any resemblance
to crowds at the Social Security Office
or the mob who line up at the BMV
is entirely identical.

I don't know exactly why, but shopping
for booze made me feel like a criminal
who would be arrested any minute.

I carried my distilled barley to the counter,
handed the clerk a credit card.
I expected him to ask for ID or at least
a fingerprint. I felt as conspicuous as
a teenager buying his first contraceptive.

When the cashier placed the bottle
in a plain brown bag, I was certain
I'd overlooked a pornographic image
on the label. The liquor store had been
relegated to the back-most part of
a large grocery store.

As I walked to the exit,
I expected customers to turn and point
their fingers at me. I made it to my car,
told myself the next time I bought hooch,
I'd get it out of town.

EPISTEMOLOGICAL DRUNK

Tonight, I've been gulping whiskey, which grew
a rat in my gut that claws and claws and claws.
I admit wasting large chunks of my life
in the name of experience? knowledge? growth?

All I ever wanted was something between me
and someone who would read poems to me
while the rest of the world topples. I tried.
I really did try to fill my hours with meaning
while looking at vacant faces.

Tonight, I sat at my desk, heard neighbors arguing,
peered down the hallway of my house at emptiness.
So, I drove to the neighborhood bar where I slump
beside people who stare into space.

I could name as many examples as there are vivid
flowers on floral wallpaper of situations in which
people disconnect or connect in all the wrong ways.

Back home, I have written no notes in the margin
of this page. I look at what I have been forthright
about. That is to say, if I could begin again,
I would start in high school to shock peers
with unadulterated honesty. I would tell them
life is a poker game, and loving someone
is a royal flush.

SAVAGERY

Jazz riffs ease into the night
like a practiced prostitute. Stumbling
from the bar, two men roar curses,
bash each other's faces. One man collapses
to the ground. The other grabs the fallen
by the hair, thumps his head against concrete,
again and again.

A siren blasts into sight. Beams flare
from the cruiser's light bar. Pushing
outside, patrons elbow each other
for the best view. Police separate
the assailants, guide them
into the cruiser's back seat. The crowd lingers
awhile then drifts back inside the bar
as the cruiser pulls from the curb.

Blood splatters reflect a neon Miller sign
announcing the place
where one man almost killed another,
the place that captured the crowd's attention
like a trapeze act gone bad.

During the brawl, music never stopped,
but someone has propped the door open,
and sorrowful notes grow louder, echo
across the parking lot. The throng steps

inside except for a man with a bucket
of water and a broom. He dilutes blood spots,
sweeps them toward the gutter, his broom
almost keeping time with the music.

BE DRUNK

Baudelaire says we should always be drunk
on wine. poetry, or virtue. Tonight I am drunk
on all three. I walk through a room, tilt
against the side of the earth, recite these lines,
think enough about goodness to feel humane.
I will go to sleep with a bottle of vodka
in my hand, a volume of Verlaine in the other.
When I awaken into the blinding light of being
sober, I will drink absinthe and be drunk again
because time taps me on the shoulder, takes
my life in bits and pieces. In a moment,
I will buddy up with Rimbaud , and we will stagger
together down the Rue de Rivoli spouting Apollinaire.
We will conduct ourselves with enough respectability
to stay upright and balanced, an occasional misstep
interrupting equilibrium, bumping us together
in an unexpected embrace. Maybe I will raise a toast
with Mallarme instead, overflow our flutes
with Louis Jadot Beaujolais Villages. We will drink
until our brains mute the tick-tock of time,
until we see minutes and hours draped like Dali's clocks
over a tree branch and desk. Or I might end up alone
in a room with a bottle of Bordeaux and a book
of Paul Valery and, contrary to his advice,
throw away the lock and key
and let the madman out of myself.

WRETCHED BLUES AND FORLORNESS OF FRIDAY NIGHT

It's Friday night, and I know nothing about love
except that it eludes me. I thought earlier I would
go to a bar, buddy up with someone, buy him a drink,
tell a raccoon story about how the critters
destroyed my roof.

This is karaoke night. Patrons will blast rafters
with pseudo singing, loudmouth wailing. Dad dragged
me to bars. Mom did too. I hated time spent
in those places, a kid making flat, salt sculptures
on shiny tables, waiting for a jukebox tune to stop
saying the same words for the fifteenth time.

I ate potato chips and drank Coke, pretended
conversations with my make-believe son
whom I would rescue from such circumstances.
I think it's normal at any age to get bored in a bar.
I just don't think I can take the sadness one more time.

I've swallowed a small dose of Klonopin and sit sullen
in my favorite chair, feeling slightly diminished
by my decision to stay home. I wonder whom
I could have met tonight: the mysterious stranger
who could have stopped my life from being miserable?
I know. I know. Only I can do that. I'm more motivated
when someone stirs the intimate air beside me.

Am I simply pining for a lost love who is in West Virginia buying heroin?

I guess it's going to be another Beethoven night on YouTube when I crawl onto the loveseat, study ceiling, listen to pretty sounds strings make. Who needs the bar? I'll be home on soft cushions, breathing easier having bypassed pretty faces and desperate daddies to write this poem about a grown man dreaming about buying a bicycle or marrying the girl who mashed his heart at a seventh grade sock-hop sixty-four years ago.

TONIGHT

I walk into a bar, tell myself
over and over you're too old
to be here. I also tell myself
you're never too old to drink.

I am looking for someone to wake me
from doldrums and depression,
someone I can tell secrets to
and not be abashed by indifference.

For that kind of search,
there is a pecking order,
and I feel at the bottom. Slow down
I tell myself. You're setting yourself up
for rejection. In this place,
glory goes to the young.
I hold my belly in and smile a lot.

I could have chosen to walk streets,
bones creaking, until exhausted,
but I chose this bar instead.

People smell desperation a mile away
and retreat. The thing is I'm tired
of holding hands with loneliness.
I'm ready to go home, take pills,
drink a Carnation Instant Breakfast,
and call it a day.

People passing me by tonight,
as if I am a waste of their time,
is an unbeautiful kind of death.
I slip off my stool, head to the exit.
I sit in my car, crushed from the dance
of discrimination humans do
before they throw you away.

TO GO AMONG THE RUINS

I'm wearing a plaid shirt and earnestness.
The plaid shirt came from a thrift shop.
The earnestness has always been there.
It's 8:30, and this loneliness thing grips me
by the wrist, leads me through most hours
of the day.

I dread careful decisions, afraid
I'll talk myself into the wrong one.
Tonight, for example, after Al-Anon,
I'm inclined to go to a bar.
It isn't that I'd love a drink.
I don't even like to drink, but
meeting someone demands being somewhere,
and as much as I dread the atmosphere of a bar,
I can sit there and hope that someone will speak
to me or make me laugh or take me into their life
to love.

I don't go to the bar after all.
I force my car homeward.
I should have gone, worn an appropriate smile,
leaned over to the person nearest me,
whispered or screamed my willingness to please
as I introduced myself. No, I wouldn't do that.
I would mind my manners, maybe buy someone a drink,
play the game, say what is required, so as not to frighten
anyone away. I wouldn't be so bold as to ask
why we are all sitting in this place, slumped over private pain.

At home, I brush my teeth, eventually
overcome stupid things my heart imagines.
I sprawl in my favorite chair and write these words,
convince myself I made the best choice
not driving into the city and into deeper despair.

CATHARTIC CEREMONY

Moonlight makes suicide attractive.
I'm not saying I'm at my end,
but I think of no gentler way to rid myself
of feelings than to walk off the cusp of the earth
which is not a hard thing to do,
since I'm surrounded by edges. I would slip
out of my clothes, wrap myself in burning
light the way I used to wrap myself
in my lover's arms. I would clear my mind
of everything but old happiness, late Autumn
days in Schiller Park when wind slapped our faces
and arrogant ducks wobbled from the pond
waiting for us to feed them popcorn. It's not hard
to find the edge of the earth when I'm already lost.
I would just keep walking until I'm free
of the first memory I ever had of someone
who mattered most.

This evening my body fell upon knives, transformed,
became emotion. I can hear my friends say, "Don't
give into yourself. Go into the house,
bolt the door. Stay away from moonlight."
Tonight, I grab a beer at the neighborhood bar,
walk the highway looking for that edge, hug the berm,
stumble over gravel. I'm out of breath, fists at my sides,
I can't walk far enough or fast enough.
I stop, look up. The moon has collapsed
behind a bank of clouds. For now, I am mostly healed,
but someday I may hurl myself off the edge
where there is no tangible grave or tombstone.

JESUS, GIVE ME A JACK AND COKE

He is not wearing a white cotton robe
and sandals. In fact, he is slightly fat
in his tight Levi's and t-shirt that reads
"Don't cross me up." He has rolled out
his best smile for Saturday night, keeps
things moving behind the bar. Ladies
like his amiable smile. Some men
do too. He seems devoted to his job.
He humbles me when I ask for a Jack
and Coke, says it's on the house.
He inspires me to follow his kind
of person, attentive, compassionate.
His enthusiasm for life
makes me want to lean on him.
Sometimes, he's helped drunks
home which he willingly does.

Tonight, though, is potluck.
Twelve regulars fill plates and settle
at the bar. The bartender uncorks
red wine, pours into each glass.
The bartender's hand trembles a little
as if a wind were blowing against it.
At closing time, he thanks them for loyalty,
tells them to have a safe trip home, says
he's glad to have played a small role
in each of their lives. He wipes down
the cedar, pine, and cypress bar
until it shines. It's been a long night,
and his feet and arthritic hands ache,
pain in his palms inescapable.

IN THE GARDEN OF NARCISSUS

These boys look into a mirror instead
of a pool, a mirror behind a row
of whiskey bottles in a neighborhood bar.
I've caught them glancing at themselves,
as if trying to figure out what they really
look like. I didn't think it mattered
to common men about self beauty,
but their quick faces in the glass
are just as intent on appearance as the
Adonis sitting next to them who cannot
tear his eyes away from self-love.

Even a peek turns me inward, all seams
of insecurity show like an inside-out sock.
I focus on whiskey bottles, true color
of their contents concealed behind big labels
and tinted glass. Like a vampire, I step back
from mirrors. Though some have said
I'm a good-looking man, I will always live
with my own *truth*.

On this particular night, I'm waiting for a man
three seats down, who is gravely unattractive,
to glimpse himself. He does, and his face tells
nothing. His eyes turn upward to the ceiling fan
as if he didn't want to know.

SITTING IN A BAR FOR HOURS ON A FRIDAY NIGHT

I've dulled a thousand synapses with Jack and Coke,
reached the limit of my salt intake with a bag
of barbecued chips. I slouch at the end of the bar
where an empty seat on either side of me invites
someone to settle. It is 12:30, deep into night
and no one has seated himself beside me.

My face wears a solemn mask. Tight skin
once attracted attention now sags
as if weighed down by a hundred stones.
I sip my drink through a short plastic straw.
I know to stay here any longer is not worth
the time, but I feel barrenness of being alone,
want to meet someone who will help me
to escape the confines of four walls.

Imagination dances on edges of a useless night.
I tell myself to go home and find refuge in writing.
Maybe all the people in here are running
from something. The majority stand in groups,
giggle and quip, seem to have arranged their bodies
in a way that makes it awkward to join them.

I walk outside to leave. It has begun to rain.
Wretched weather drips from the overhang.
If I could only stop the ache of wanting
to be with someone, I could ease into this spring
night without graceless grief that comes
from expecting hit-or-miss romance.

BODY TRUTH

By midnight, sweet scent of cologne has faded
to a hint of itself. Young men in the crowd
go out of their way not to look at older men
sitting at the bar. Over-amplified music,
reminiscent of disco, pounds the walls.

I'm absorbed by my reflection in the mirror
in front of me, think I see myself for the first time
the way others do. Behind me,
a man holds another man in his arms.
Feelings flood me, something about opening up,
letting someone in.

A few more drinks and people become featureless.
A few more drinks and I will not be able to explain
to a cop how I became a broken man,
the one whose dad took a power saw to his heart.

Meanwhile, I'm arranging my blurred look
to nonchalance. When I walked
through the door, I knew I was in the wrong
place. I have a talent for revealing
my loneliness. It starts in the eyes. I may
as well have stayed home and read a book.
I have barely exchanged looks with anyone,
and when I do, they glance away.

I stand, work my way through half-naked torsos,
drag queens, elderly men. It feels as if
I'm leaving a human junkyard, a place where
music, colored lights, and liquor promise
instant paradise, but deliver only
pocketsful of sadness.

THE DRAG QUEEN'S BINGO GAME

Sunday night is bingo night at the bar.
I arrive at 9 o'clock, take my usual seat
at the far end out of sight of the stage
and unkind and malicious humor
of drag queen, Frida Love, who hosts.

It takes hours for her to call numbers,
because after each draw, she spews patrons
with campy venom, making bitchiness
sound like sweet talk.

At first break, I hope she won't spot me
hiding around the corner. I have never met her.
This is my first time at the bar on bingo night.
Sure enough, she sights me, sashays
in my direction, oozing sex in a mauve, off-shoulder,
sequin evening dress, large blonde wig.
Perfectly applied makeup gives her elegance
she has apparently striven for.

She asks why I'm not playing bingo.
I don't answer. I simply stare. She is beautiful,
close enough to smell her perfume. She has left
the nasty, spiteful persona on stage. This is
a gentle person wanting to please. When I speak,
I tell her how attractive she is. She looks into
my eyes, tells me I am beautiful. Then

she runs her fingers over my hair.
When her break ends, she pulls me to the center
of the bar, places a bingo card in front of me.

It is near midnight, time for the last game.
I have drunk enough Jack and Coke that
the game has become surreal. Through
blurred vision I can tell that I have a lucky card.

I yell, BINGO, raise my arm. She calls me
to the stage, overjoyed that I have won
the big prize of the evening, a boombox
with a CD player. Holding me in a clutch,
she insists someone take our picture.

When I start to leave through the back exit,
she follows me to the patio. We stand peering
into each other's eyes, quiet as stars, staring.
It is a satisfying moment of inebriated haze.
Within a milieu of comfortable vagueness,
she takes my hand, whispers "come back."

THANKSGIVING EVENING

By six o'clock, family obligations
have been disposed of, a version of
civility dusted off for the holiday.
Dishes placed in the washer,
tablecloths folded and shelved,
chairs stacked and removed to storage,
relatives sort for coats, don them,
head home with leftovers.
I have a different destination.

I've just eaten with family, drifted
on casual conversation, held onto
predictable security. Now, because
of a fierce need to neutralize longing
for you, obliterate obsession.
I'm heading to a bar.

I pull into the lot, bewildered
by lack of cars. I thought this place
would be packed. The bartender,
one other patron and I, the only
occupants. I order a Jack and Coke,
wonder if I'm slowly becoming a drunk,
but no, this is just a temporary stopping
off, an attempt to desensitize myself
to the very place where we first met.

Everywhere I look, I see something
about us. Somehow, being here isn't
working. Though I sent you away,
wanting you back is claws tearing
at my brain.

Another Jack and Coke, and I'm out
of here. I tap my fingers on the bar.
Our relationship was beyond repair.
Although I say that, I can never
remember a time I didn't want to be
with you. My hands will stay
in my lap before I ever touch
another person the same way
I touched you. I don't know
what that means. I only know
what I feel.

I push away from the bar, think
it is finally safe to go home
to an empty house. I have had
enough of memory. That is all
there is.

EMPTY TOWN

I'm sitting in a bar on Christmas Eve.
Why not? I have nowhere else to go.
I expected to encounter a crowd
I could get lost among, but the place
is almost vacant. One other patron droops
over a double shot. The bartender prances
back and forth from boredom, and I want more
than a drink and fatuous conversation.

Suddenly, I'm in the shadow of someone
who swaggers through the door and sits down
beside me. I am half drunk. He leans close,
compliments me on my cologne. My skin
prickles, and I lean next to his ear, whisper
words that help him know me, the excuse
for contact. I invite him home. He says,
"That will cost extra." which hurls innocence
to the gutter, blackens the eye of possibility
like the punch from a prostitute.

I turn my back on my drink and him,
slip out the door while he looks away.

In the car I think about personal details
we exchanged, and how it all came down
to embarrassing negotiation.

I swerve from the parking lot,
head down Parsons Avenue, wishing I had paid
attention to the many rumors of
his bad intentions.

NEW YEAR'S EVE, 2018

I lift a Collins glass of Jack and Coke.
The clock stalks minutes until midnight.
The bar has more people packed into it
than I suspect the owner ever dreamed of.
It's a night to be in behind windows against
which rain pounds like a maniac's tears,
competes with amped-up thumping
of a dance tune.

Bottles tipped, glasses drained, camaraderie
suffuses the crowd. At such times, I feel
as if the earth moves away from me
a drink at a time, as if I am slipping
down a hillside, trying to hold on
to equilibrium. I envy the drunk
who clears his throat, spits in the gutter,
teeters home unbothered by an empty bed.
Others have waited all year to be satisfied
with a random kiss.

My teeth are all mine, skin still firm,
and I smell of an expensive cologne.
I have three college degrees that say I talk
and write well, but when the clock bongs twelve,
I would put what's left of my life on the line
to lie down with someone who would not
eat my heart for breakfast.

At five minutes to twelve I slip out the back exit
to forgo imminent pandemonium, to avoid
faces turning to see me single and burdened
by the weight of unrelenting loneliness.

I DO NOT SING WHEN I DRINK

I've drunk too much at the bar, way over
my limit. The world fuzzes enough
to tolerate. Bottles lined against a mirror
are glass bowling pins filled with gold
intoxication. I drink Jack and Coke
a tranquilizing sip at a time. Patrons straddle
stools on either side of me, drone opening
lines, defeated, disappear out the door
or onto the dance floor where their arms
become snakes reaching for rhythms.

I wait for infatuation to spin into my life
like colored lights rotating from the ceiling,
the much anticipated magical second.
It takes skill to avoid instant romance.

Number nine sits down beside me, green eyes,
a wide smile. I order another Jack and Coke.
Number nine sweats from dancing, is swift
in the art of aggression, introduces himself,
but by now, I want to avoid a one-night stand.
I stare straight ahead to dodge conversation.

I glance in the mirror. Bottles have blurred.
Haze of inebriation and subdued lighting
erase twenty years from my face. At that moment,
fogged by whiskey, I slide from my stool,

seek balance, my body guessing distance
to the door. I linger on the patio, reluctant
to drive. A sudden hand on my shoulder
and green eyes guides me to a wooden bench.
He sits beside me, and I slur "What
happened to me in there?" His hand finds
mine. "You drank too much. You'll be fine.
I'll get you water." He rises. "I'm sorry
I resisted your company," I say. He leans
close to my ear, says "I'm more
than a one-night stand."

FORCE OF HEART

I'm a little bit hunched on a bar stool,
trying to gather the nerve to buy you
a drink. Your unlined face smiles at me,
but since you're bartending, you say
it will have to wait until after work.
I down one Jack and Coke and many more
Cokes, waiting to see if you will actually
take up my offer. At eight o' clock,
you disappear to the back room
to exchange money trays with the
oncoming bartender.

The place crowds with much banter
and jovial noise. When I think
you have sneaked out the back door,
you finally show up and sit down beside me.
I admit to you that it is the first time
I've ever offered to buy someone a drink.
You seem a little dumbfounded by that.

I learned earlier in the evening
you have a second job you'll be going to
within the hour. I thank you for staying
around for the drink.   Beneath generosity,
I'm asking myself what I want?
Maybe nothing more than to have someone
make me feel I count.

I know we will shake hands at the end,
but I also know I want to touch you
without sexual intent. I want to lay
my hand on yours without the handshake.
Our talk is not small talk, but it is sparse,
generously punctuated with silence.
You finish your beer, stand up.
We do shake hands after all.

When you've left, I find myself wishing
we could have shuttered in the cold
November night together.

BE CAREFUL, LEO

He's sitting beside me on a bar stool.
I think he's a stoic figure who wants
to keep to himself, but I'm wrong.
He leans toward me, thin hair, worn
face with grooves of hard living.
He starts to tell me about World War l,
World War II, the Korean War, Vietnam,
jungles, that Vietnamese eat
anything and everything. He's seen
a monkey stripped of skin, wiggling
from life before being devoured
by hungry people. He pontificates
about real estate purchases that will
make him rich if he grabs sale-houses
in the South End.

He flips out his phone to a picture of his
twenty-something-year-old girlfriend.
She's black and comely. He's white and sixty.
He thinks they could not be more suited.

I don't buy him a drink. I do offer him
my cheese puffs which he gladly accepts.
He thinks I'm a wonderful person because
I've listened to his gibberish for over an hour.
I lean on an elbow, my face toward his
as if he were the most important person
I've ever heard.

He keeps ordering doubles, and I keep
wondering when he'll quit talking and go home.
I want to tell him I've had enough, but
I've been raised to believe I should tolerate
whatever annoys me with patience.

He talks about gentrification of the South End,
wants to move from ritzy Clintonville
down here, become part of the upsweep
that's occurring in this part of Columbus.

Finally, he pays for his last drink,
shoulders his backpack, and leaves.
I yell after him, "Be careful, Leo."

As much as I don't want to be by myself
in the bar, I'm glad he's gone. It is good
that he interrupted my life for a while
with his stories. I had nothing better to do
than surrender to another human's loneliness.

FAILED PROMISES OF THE FLESH

All evening, I go slow on Jack and Coke,
pay bar bills for men along the rail.
I'm not broke yet, but my pocket is filled
with one dollar bills. There are white men
and black men in the room, and I have been
caught looking at each of them.
Whiskey swirls in my stomach.
I try to be dignified while being ignored,
tell the bartender to pour me another.

It's karaoke night. Some patrons are whores
of the mic, slobbering off-key reverberations
while others seal the gap between amateur
and professional.

It's an hour before closing.
A guy named Gage sits next to me.
I stare into his eyes like a child in need
of a hug. He doesn't want to catch on,
nor do other patrons who go outside
for a smoke or cross their indifference
at the ankles.

I want to leave, go home and write.
Slouching away from the bar toward the door,
I do not say goodbye.

Chill of winter stuns as I unlock my car,
drive home thinking the ones who drank
every drop of liquor I bought, faced away
from me, a wall of backs, any one of which
could have turned, kept me from believing
God didn't care.

FRIDAY NIGHT GATHERING OF FELLOWS AT A FAVORITE WATERING HOLE

Some seem never to have left their seats
since the last time I was here. These
regulars turn toward my entrance, nod
a stiff hello, turn back to nurse drinks.

It's going on seven o'clock. Soon
muscle boys and old men with money
will amble in, imbibe slow hours of booze
and sexual negotiation.

I settle on a stool at the end of the bar.
No one sits either side as if I give off vibes
I prefer isolation. I guzzle Jack and Coke,
chase it with plain Coke. Fingers wrapped
around sweat on my empty glass signals
the bartender for a Jack and Coke refill.
This time, I sip, glance in the mirror
behind the bar. I'm moody as a silk scarf
twisting in the wind. The mirror shows
white hair, green eyes, a craving for
companionship.

The pain of losing you never quits, but
if you walked in right now, I would remember
how opposite we are, turn away without a word.
Friends say I come to this particular bar hoping
you will come through the door.

Upon an elevated stage, a stripper slips
out of black paratrooper pants, peels off
yellow t-shirt, gyrates a blue G string.
Patrons slide dollar bills under his waistband.
I look away from those drowning in desperation.

I reach for the tab, head out, unable to leave
even half the feeling of hollowness behind.

STRIPPER

You dance tonight under canary yellow
light at The Holy Bird Bar. You might think
you own the sun because of the golden glow
on your skin as you strip away clothes
a piece at a time. The stage is too small
for the song's beat, but you move
self-assured in contained space.
At twenty-nine, your build needs no further
enhancement. It is, as they say, ripped,
alive with sexual suggestion. You've said
people on the street ignore you, but tonight
you have full attention. There are bursts of
applause as you grab between your legs.
Perhaps you think this is the most important
night of your life. The room is alive
with appreciation. Perhaps at this moment
you think you will never age, that
you can savor youth forever. Remembering
right moves is involuntary. Incessant
practices have lead to perfection, to sensual
aplomb.

Afterwards, you reward yourself
with a cigarette, a towel to wipe the sweat.
You work through the crowd, letting them
touch you, letting them stuff dollars beneath
your waistband. A few will ask for hookups.

You go home too bed, your heart perhaps
crying out for yet one more second
of Saturday night satisfaction.

A WRONG END TO THE NIGHT

I'm a man with white hair from his forehead
to the nape of his neck. What can I expect
except rejection in a bar where youth flaunts,
takes itself for granted. This is what
I'm thinking as I circle the block, looking
for a parking spot at The Holy Bird Saloon.

The same people slouched in this bar
twenty-five years ago with different names,
different faces. I perch on a stool, watch
young men fluff their plumage, hug each other
slightly off-balance. I slide a few coins
into the game machine, force myself
to swallow Jack and Coke I don't want.
I take small sips because I hope
the drink lasts until I fall asleep
with my head and arms limp on the bar or
until someone seats himself beside me
and siphons off a bit of solitude.

When it's almost two in the morning,
the cardboard people ask for a last drink.
The bartender lingers near my end
of the bar, moves away, comes back.
All evening we haven't talked
or exchanged names. What I really want
to ask him is "Do you happen to know
what happened to my life?"

He is wiping the bar with a damp rag.
I lift my glass out of the way.
When I get up to leave, he says
"Have a safe trip home." I thank him
and absolutely hate that he isn't coming with me.

III

GOD TRICKS

*Never shall I forget those moments
that murdered my God and my
soul and turned my dreams to
ashes.*

-Elie Wiesel

*Is man merely a mistake of God's?
Or God merely a mistake of man?*

-Friedrich Nietzsche

WHICH GOD?

How many gods have you counted today?
There's the god of the streets, the god of rain
and snow, the God without a tongue who
never answers. There's the God you pay for
through television evangelists, the God
whose angels make love behind his back,
the God who sits on a golden throne eyeballing
all of time and space. The list of gods goes on.
It's a regular smorgasbord.

You say you are contented with one God,
the personal one only you know about?
If that is true, put your money in the plate
and carry on.

I have watched you preen for church, pray
that your hat was on straight, dogma inviolate.
I've seen you admire mahogany benches,
a new burgundy runner down the main aisle,
the freshly painted crucifix. I've also seen
that dim shadow of doubt in your eye
as if to ask are you praying to the right God
after all? The question spins in your head.
You've circled around it ever since the day
you were able to think for yourself.

A steeple bell rings, restores faith
and all of its cliches.
You stand on church steps and socialize,
relegate God to the wings for a while. Sometimes,
it's a jungle out there you tell your friend,
but weren't the flowers at the altar beautiful?

UNDERSTANDING SUCH THINGS AS GOD

Pushing upwards of millions of years,
He looks good, damn good for His age.
At least He is not tattooed, sporting
sagging pants.

Should I speak first? What is the proper
etiquette when addressing God?
My mind contains so many questions
it's hard not to sputter. He places
a massive hand on my shoulder, and
sensations, not words infuse my mind.

This might be a once-in-a-lifetime
opportunity. I'm nervous as I would be
on a blind date. Since He doesn't speak
in words, I'm hesitant how to communicate.
He nods as if to say go ahead.

I sort out one question from the many
I want to ask. Does He know
what is in everyone's head at all times?
His hand on my shoulder assures
He does. Just as I'm getting used
to this whole celestial ballgame,
He dissolves like snow in sunlight,
or a raindrop on the lip of a garden
flower, and I am caught up again
in incurable doubt and the spiritual
drift of humanity.

GOD NEVER KISSED BOBBY WAKEFIELD

Bobby mutters around in the middle
of words he can't articulate, his
incoherent language a drool onto a white bib.
He gurgles careful sounds in his throat,
alive with personal meaning but empty
as silence to the listener.

His hands, permanently bent at the wrist,
resemble chicken claws that tear air
to communicate. He can't even speak
of his grief or what it means to have a face
frozen in calm desperation.

Crooked legs trip along the same daily route
of South End streets. Neighbors accommodate
with patience, compassion, speak to him
as if he were a regular person just stopping by
for a chat, their commitment to his welfare explicit.
People step close, embrace his hands with theirs,
offer small talk.

Bobby's face doesn't etch laugh lines.
Skin around his eyes stays inert, smooth
as polished stone. Sometimes, he wanders
into my parents' confectionery on Barthman
Avenue, and my dad jokes with him,
and Bobby makes excited noises that suggest
a laugh. He never had a spouse or anyone
linked to romantic love.

Maybe at night he closes his eyes, pretends
God has mended his brokenness, but when
he awakens, he knows once again that
he can't even comb his own hair.

JOHNNY GORDON LETS GO WITH GOD

Look God, I'm serious about breaking away
from the need for you to watch my back.
For years, I've trusted, but I'm sick of silence
when I ask you loudly to alleviate pain
and cruelty from every relationship
I've ever embraced.

The public protects your image, says
you hold arms open to whomever wants
to be held. I'm leery of such an offer,
frightened of threadbare possibility
you, in robes white as popcorn, will not
return my love or rescue me after all.

You've barely glanced in my direction,
glowed a little like a candle and disappeared.
You have almost completely ignored me
since I leaned out of a Ferris wheel seat
one autumn evening and caught sight
of your existence. Since then, I have
swung my arms wide, almost hit myself
in the eye to get your attention.

Your caring eludes me. You're not a ghost.
You don't evaporate. I know you're there
in the afternoon or at 3 a.m. in the morning.

The problem is, I'm wrestling
with a desire to see your face, the look
that will tell if you're satisfied with me.

My words are awkward. I stumble over
my own coattails when I walk your way.
You are full of grace, and I have demonstrated
a disgusting lack of it.

I have not flung the door shut on you.
We could probably settle all of this
over a cup of coffee, but I don't drink coffee.
Instead, and I'm not being sarcastic,
an enormous hug would do.

ICONOCLAST

The church is empty, and I have been lured
inside by loneliness, feel as if I have trespassed,
even though the door is unlocked.
I holler hello down the nave
just to hear my voice defy consecrated silence.
Apparently, all the angels have gone home.

As I walk to the front, confusion darkens
my mind about innocence of God and Jesus.
Is God a psychopathic do-gooder,
his son nothing more than a thought
that happened into holiness by popular hallucination?

I bend to knees. Respect shifts
into neutral as I bask in the gilded spit
and shine of Christianity.

I would die for the real God,
never adequately explained to me.
Faults, deficits, fifty afflictions
of my soul stand me so close to endless
fires I confess not to be a candidate
for the eternal plan of happiness.

Closing the door, I slip to the street, feel very small
about what I can do to amend half-faith
I have toppled like a sacred statue.

I stand outside looking up at the steeple,
awed as a child by nothing more than height.

ON A COUNTRY ROAD I LEARNED THERE IS NO GOD

After the second vodka gimlet, I drive
from a Parsons Avenue bar until
the scenery becomes rural. I tromp the accelerator
for several miles, ease up to legal speed,
and pull over to a transmission tower.
Against the headrest, I lean back, sob.
I wipe away tears with the back of my hand.

An oncoming car slows.
The driver wants to know if I need help.
I tell him I'm good, thank him. I watch
in the rear view mirror until he disappears.
 I see bright lights of the casino
across the field, start the engine.

My tires spit gravel as I pull back
onto the road. I see my reflection
in a side window, or is it God's face?
I have stared into his eyes before.
He was dying even then, but I had
nowhere else to go. I was alone in my head.
He tells me how I will feel better if I walk
among the birds and trees. I think he is lying.
His omniscience goes only so far
when all he has to offer is birds and trees,
when he cannot ease my fear of everything

from moonlight to knives. I have screamed
prayers, begged him to lift the weight
of unrequited love. I make a u-turn
and head home. Tonight, I am an unbeliever.
He will not catch me praying again.

AT WOODRUFF AND HIGH

I'm attending a poetry reading
at Saint Stephen's church on The Ohio
State University campus. I arrive
a half hour early. The first one there,
I amble among Church paraphernalia:
a crib, collection plate, chalice.
A large stained-glass crucifix hangs
slightly behind and above the pulpit.
Sunset glows through side windows.
I know any sound I make echos
up to high ceilings no matter how loud
or soft I speak. I do nothing to feel saintly
except pull open wooden doors and walk in,
but the very air sanctifies me. I feel special
the way I do when I dress formally.

For a moment, I think of the church as God's
architecture, his blueprint for a place away
from pandemonium. I think about love
and wonder if I will ever find this kind
of peace with another person. I walk around,
don't touch anything because it all seems
beyond reach of a secular hand.

When other people arrive, the ambiance
dilutes with hellos and amiable greetings.
People fill pews at the front of the Nave,

and the poetry begins. I throw many glances
at the stained-glass cross during the reading,
remember how nothing mattered for a while
except standing alone in the church.

DO ANGELS MAKE LOVE?

Do angels make love, tangle their hands
in each others hair, bring longing to the point
of ecstasy? Do angels beat their wings and say
I love you as many times as people do
without meaning it?

I walk under milk-white clouds, knowing angels
sometimes hide from humans to avoid hearing stories
of tattered hearts.

Angels must be full of wisdom or, to sum it up,
beg us to give up our sadness.

I have talked to angels, not quite
walked down the street with them
but in a swatch of air saw their faces,
heard their voices answer my questions.
I told them how I have become a shell
wearing clothes, trying to discover love
I can only find in poetry. They did not turn
away, said they understood I was kicking
around dead dreams.

Without warning they intertwined like lovers,
showed me how easy it is to be tender.

And then, as if they were a flash of deer
in a forest, disappeared. The winter day
lay before me. I could see smoke rising
from the chimney of my house, indefinite
as angels' breath.

JESSE WANTS TO HELP YOU

I misread the Methodist sign board
as I pass the church. I think
it says Jesse wants to help you. Will
you let him? Part of the problem is
I'm reading it from peripheral vision,
from a car speeding past it too fast
to take a good look. It actually says
Jesus wants to help you. Will you
let him? I am more interested when
I think someone named Jesse is
offering help. Before I learn the truth,
I begin to elevate Jesse to a higher level
of human being, thinking he is at least
a do-gooder if not an outright altruist. Yet,
how can the holy proposition contain
a commoner. Until I recognize my mistake,
I want to meet Jesse, ask him just how
he plans to save the world. The thing is,
how much instant faith I have in someone
I don't even know just because his name
appears on the church marquee.

Maybe all belief begins with a mistake.
My mistake is innocent. I don't mean
to slight Jesus. It's just that hope skewered
on a split second while I thought someone
new was filling in for Mary's son. The next

time I passed the church, I drove slower,
saw that God was not moving someone else
into Jesus's place.

The question is, would I have trusted anyone
whose name happened to be on the marquee?
Check it off as an unholy error or, better yet,
a renewal of confidence in common man.

ALLEY ANIMALS

You slouch against the back of a garage
in an alley where rape and murder are
commonplace, take a drag on your cigarette,
swallow the smoke. You're fourteen years old.
Your parents have shared drugs with you
until you puke. You idolize your father.
A week from today, you will find him dead
at the kitchen table from an overdose
of heroin.

You don't belong to a gang,
but you have plenty of buddies who hang
with you. Most are dealers, hopheads themselves.
One of them shoulders up to you,
your cue to hand over payment for a gram
of smack. The whole exchange is as graceful
as communion. You pocket the dope and dance
out another Marlboro, pack it, veteran
of the nicotine ritual since you were nine.
You whisper, "Later, man," disappear to the street,
eager to intoxicate your veins.

You enter the squalid house you share
with two other addicts, shut your bedroom door,
tie-wrap your arm with a shoelace, and
spoon-cook the powder to a liquid.

An array of needles protrude from a bowl
like a bouquet of silver bicycle spokes.
Your vein has popped, and you inject.
You flop on the bed at the peak of pleasure,
feeling sure God has walked away
from your wasted life.

BAD WORDS

His mind did not dabble in holiness.
At one time, he would have bled for his God,
but his notebook was his own confessional.
In it he admitted an attraction to the woman
who talked to him once a week through a metal
screen with a cloverleaf pattern. She had no clue
he dragged his heart through silence when
she whispered of her adulterous sin. The notebook
contained words he breathed only upon its pages,
words that brush-stroked adoration and unspoken
love into existence.

He watched her from his window when she crossed
the street to enter the church. Other times,
from his window, he studied her pushing
her two-year-old son in his pram.
He had shot himself in the heart
with a soft bullet of guilt, couldn't stop craving her.

On this particular day, he saw her leave her house
across the street, disappear through the entrance
to the church beneath his window. In the confessional,
he ripped the clerical collar from his neck,
pronounced words that had never come from his mouth
before. She arose from her knees, having learned
how he loved her. He apologized and did not say more.

She left, went home, planted nasturtiums, working soil
as if depth of her fingers in the dirt could bury embarrassment.
The priest dropped his clerical collar on the floor
of the confessional, didn't bother to pick it up.

Days later, he left town dressed in civilian clothes,
the notebook concealed in his suitcase beneath his cassock.
Regret scalded his conscience. Secondhand prayer offered
no solace. He drove to a small neighboring town,
hands gripping the wheel like a death hold on redemption.

METAPHYSICS OF THE SKY

I once looked up at the sky and thought,
what is the sky? Is it just a piece of blue
that happens to be bigger than anything else,
repeating itself over and over ad infinitum?
And which part of the sky is heaven?
I cannot contemplate magnitude of answers
that would satisfy such questions.

Maybe I have to settle for a bird's sky
designated by limits of oxygen. Is that
when sky turns into atmosphere, when birds
curve back to earth?

Anytime can be a sky. There is winter sky,
summer sky, stormy sky, sky that becomes
a wall when fog descends. These difficult
questions tell science to step aside. Real
answers call for impossible information.

I think if the sky were alive, it would promise
to be there forever, but I'll finish that sentence
by saying it's a dangerous promise. I sink
into deep silence when I think about destruction.
Man has domesticated the moon, devoured stars.
There will never be a privilege to approach the sun,
or it, too, would become one of man's collectibles.

The sky is too big to fit into a coffin.
Public passion for unhappy moments would
with pleasure phone home to announce it's death,
if the day ever comes when man can find a way
to wage war and wipe out the sky with one blue gasp.

HOLY

What right do I have to feel holy,
but sometimes I do, as if encircled
by an ethereal sphere. It does not come
from abstinence, self-flagellation, or
following God's plan. When I write,
I become encapsulated in extravagant
Christianity, a non translatable condition
not to be confused with liturgy.
When I write, the boundaries of time dissolve,
the world disappears until I invent it again.

I have deep faith in words. They help me
identify beliefs. The Holiness I speak of
is neither a halo around my head nor reward
for unaccompaning the devil into hell.
The burn to create is my religion,
theology that teaches the power
of selecting the right word.

Church is anywhere I hold pen and paper.
A poem is a prayer. I cannot defend
my holiness beyond this description.
It only falls upon me when I write.
Time and place become one dimensional.
Everything surrounding me shifts
out of focus. I stray from the real world,
hover over paper, ready to astound myself
with the surprise of unanticipated and
unexpected language.

STONING THEOLOGY

God can't just meander eternity
without a plan for us. Or is it true
we have to invent our own path,
our own stratagems for getting through
the tangle of life?

It doesn't help that angels keep
rearranging furniture of belief.
Just as I'm ready to sit down
on a chair of commitment, it's pulled
out from under me like a third-rate clown
act.

My mind overflows with catechism, think
I'm beginning to generate faith when
the devil shoots me in the brain with doubt.

Well, let's talk about the devil. I've romanced
him, didn't find it demeaning or undignified.
In fact, I enjoyed the tryst. I displayed
elaborate dysfunction, hung over the fiery pit
without being burned. Can it be I'm nothing
more than a heathen, someone who wants
to make a deity of night, fall headfirst
into narcotic moonlight?

Hell is more than the evermore of fire.
I stepped into it barefoot and naked,
wandered over boiling coals, took
comfort in burnless surprise.
I didn't turn to ash, slogged closer
and closer to flames that did not blacken
me or my soul the way condemnation
would have on the sidewalks of heaven.

IV

TEMPORARY AFFECTIONS

Sometimes, when we least expect it, we catch a glimpse of someone, a face, perhaps only a smile, and our heart latches on and will not let go.

-Regan Walker

The world needs more love at first sight.

-Maggie Stiefvater, Shiver

THE MEXICANS

Five men shoulder bundles of shingles
to a place on the lawn in front of the house.
I stand in the opening to the garage
and watch them work: Macho men
guard their masculinity with a fist
if given a wrong look.

I signal the supervisor for a word.
He strolls over to me. I take him
into the house and show him where
the ceiling has been leaking. He assures
when they're finished putting on the new roof,
the leaks will disappear. I follow him back outside.
He continues to unload shingles from the truck.

One of the workers is particularly good looking,
reminds me of someone from my past
who promised not to break my heart, but did.
This worker's lithe body strains under the weight
of a bundle, but he continues to do his share.
The whole time the men work, they jabber Spanish.
There are smiles in their voices and an explicit
camaraderie.

Rain begins, so the supervisor tells me
they will be back in the morning to finish.
I watch them prepare to leave, follow
the attractive one from the corner of my eye.

I think he looks at me too, but only with suspicion.
Soon, they are packed and drive away.
I hope to see his lovely brown face tomorrow.

AFTER I GOT MY NEW ROOF

Five Mexican workers replace my roof.
The youngest and handsomest worker loads
bundles of shingles onto the ladder-lift that
transports them to the roof. From the living
room window, I watch him until the last bag
is lifted. The ubiquitous noise of tearing and
ripping permeates the ceiling.

Several hours later, rhythmic sounds
of pounding hammers replace the ripping racket.
Pieces of debris continually fall to the lawn.
The work team is remarkably focused, go about
their tasks like programmed robots.

I mosey outside to speak with the supervisor
whose English is only fairly fluent, but he is friendly
and likable. I look up at the roof and compliment
him and his workers on a superior job.

Back in the house, I continue to watch the cleanup.
By now, I have become familiar with the men's faces
and body movements.. They have become a stopgap
family for a few lonely hours. I want to invite them
into the house and spew out words that will make them
friends. I am embarrassed to want this to happen,
and I hope desperation does not show in my eyes.

I return to the house and to the window.
The men have packed their gear, and truck engines rev.
After they pull away, there is nothing for me to look at
except immaculate lawn and nothing for me to hear
except silence that keeps getting closer and closer.

APRIL 27, 2019 EVENING WISH

Exactly an hour and a half after
workers have finished replacing my roof,
it starts to rain. God has such a way with humor.
It's 5:30, and I'm on the edge of Saturday night
with a personal pizza in the oven. Somewhere,
along the line, I bought into the myth that on Friday
and Saturday nights the city is out having a good time.

While I wait for the pizza to heat,
I watch rain drizzle through dogwood blossoms
and wish mom were alive, so we could share
the satisfaction of having a new roof.
Tonight, I feel like an ant on a leaf
of loneliness crossing a river of solitude.

It's not quite twilight. I look outside, and
everything is April green and still,
except for fine rain. I have only four dollars,
so I can't go to the bar, order a Jack and Coke,
which is $5.50, and get an insipid conversation
going with another malcontent. What difference
does it make now to tell someone about my empty bed
or that I've never slept all night beside a man?
By morning I will have forgotten
that I even said these things,
that I pleaded with myself not to scream
into the night for a knock at the door.

THE SHAPE OF ANONYMITY

I am leaving the Ohio State fairgrounds,
pass a large tent. Outside lights are doused,
but one work light inside the tent still burns.
A man is closing down for the night.
His silhouette shows through the canvas,
a shadowy shape of solitude who thinks
for certain he is alone. He seems to be packing
a bag or trunk. I take out my camera and snap
a photo of his outline on the side of the tent.
The scene is so ethereal; it's as if he were packing
to leave the earth.

The rest of the fairgrounds is relatively dark
and quiet which underscores the dramatic effect
of this tableau. I keep walking from the grounds,
thinking that when he shuts off that last light,
he will disappear, and I will never know
what his worst fear is or his happiest moment.

For a few seconds, I feel affection
for this stranger on the other side of the screen,
someone without details, a shape that shared
loneliness with me without ever knowing it.

YOU SURPRISE ME WITH YOUR INTEREST

You dropped everything you were doing
to wait on me in Kroger's Bakery.
I told you I wanted to order a sheet cake
with a picture of the cover of my newest book
for a book-launch party. We discussed prices,
sizes. Abruptly, you asked if I am an author.
I said yes, and you asked to buy my book.
I told you I would bring you a copy
when I come back to place my order.
You smiled and thanked me.

Was there more in that smile than friendliness?
Imagination went to work immediately.
I was intuitively convinced you wanted me
to feel something more.

I have no idea what will happen
when I give you the book. Will you ask me
for my email address to send your reaction?
Will that be the beginning or end of us?

I can't forget your eyes
opening wide to me. When I return,
maybe you'll only stretch out your hand,
and we'll shake, or maybe the two of us
will hit the road, never return
to a loneliness I have so far survived.

PAPER AND INK

I drive to Micro Center tonight to purchase
paper and ink. Mist from January rain hazes
the windshield. A red snake of brake lights
crawls for miles ahead. The heater's warmth
makes me drowsy, want to pull into myself
and sleep. Hungry for silence, I leave the radio
off, satisfied to hear the monotonous swish
of rain blinked away by wipers.

From Bethel Road, I turn into the parking lot.
Inside, I grab handles of a basket I will put
everything in I want to buy. I find the aisle
for ink and paper, and a handsome young clerk
with blonde streaks in his brown hair strolls over
to me and says he likes my hair. I'm so surprised
by the compliment that I forget to thank him.
He appears to be the kind of guy who receives
compliments but doesn't often give them.

Such a little thing, his several words, saves a day
I had let collapse into depression. After
he helps me find paper and ink, we stand
together a few seconds. Yes, for just a few seconds,
but it that short time, we find each other's smile
and something else like a promise not to forget
how that moment felt.

ONE-SIDED

I look all afternoon on the dating site,
not liking anything I've seen, and then
someone comes to push snow away
from the driveway, and I fall in love.
Not exactly a magazine model but
with black bearded jawline, handsome.
My heart pushes back something electric.
My flesh whispers dirty little stories
to itself. Then I wait for shame to set in.
How can I want someone so fast?
Fluttering in my brain, equal to three shots
of vodka, makes me intrepid, but not
enough to step forward, risk reducing
another person to embarrassment.
Call it passion in passing or desire
at a glance. I pay him forty dollars for snow
removal and a hint at how the right person
causes a blood rush.

The driveway is clean as if swept by a broom.
But what now of the face that disappeared,
drained away as he turned off the road?

I enter the house, thinking life of the mind
is audacious. I see it's beginning to snow again.
Something in me has become fragile as smoke.
Something in me aches to repeat the scenario.

AT FLYERS PIZZA AND SUB SHOP

He wears a gold chain and the smugness
of youth. Ring and bracelet round out
his ensemble of jewelry. Because it is
a warm, early April day, he sports black
sleeveless t-shirt, well-worked biceps.

She perches across from him, turns profile.
I see her lovely face, its smooth contours.
Her hair hangs long, brown, and straight.
She has the beauty most women envy.

I try not to stare at them,
to detect flaws which I do when
they step outside to smoke.
With a turn of my head, I see them
out the front window. They could be
high school age or a little older.
I think I want them
porcelain perfect, or do I?
Truth is I resent their youth,
good looks, am a bit satisfied to see
porcelain crack. I assume they have sex.
That eliminates innocence.
Maybe I don't want them to have clean hearts.
Maybe I want glass to break, mercury to spill.

When I'm ready to leave, I try not to show effort
struggling from the booth.

CHEF

The Waffle House sign, yellow as a gigantic bumblebee,
sits in an open field around the corner from where I live.
Out of convenience, I eat there often, even though the air
and menus feel greasy.

I like the evening waitress best.. Her black eyeliner
is the youngest part of her face, but what fascinates me
most is the chef whose face I've never seen. He focuses
on the grill and only the grill, never turns profile,
never turns around toward customers. I assume
his young age from knotted hair, slim build, and
low-slung pants. He stands straight, never slumps.
His knife and spatula flash efficiency. It is as if
he has been instructed not to turn around.
Is there a deeper reason for him to turn away?
Is he scarred? Is he trying to stay anonymous?

I want to speak to him. I want to offer a tip
for his good work, but I will not intrude on
the milieu in which he has cocooned himself.
Sometimes, I want to yell, "Turn around!
Resolve the mystery!"

I'm struggling not to want to know him better,
working against an impetuous desire to wait
for him after work, to see him reveal
an attempted smile or the saddest face. Would

he clinch fists at my intrusion, think I'm stalking?
Perhaps it's best to let him remain invisible.

I have memorized the back of him, watched him
daily, a one-sided Phoenix rising from flames
of his sacred grill, distance between us a waffle away.

ANATOMY OF A MOMENTARY PASSION

Many times, first impressions precipitate
instant crushes. Like tonight at the Olive Garden,
the waiter's beautiful hands balanced a tray
while the blaze of his blue eyes addled me.
He knew his effect, stretched perfectly-formed lips
into a shy smile. I did not blurt wrong words
from desire to know him. I simply ordered rigatoni,
marinara sauce, and a side salad with ranch dressing.
I watched him turn away with balance
and grace of Nureyev. I never get tired of
falling in love in public, wonder if someone
as stunning as this waiter ever gets bored
with his perfection. If I compliment him on looks,
I would break the tenuous connection,
probably just part of his job.

What do I want? What do I desire
from this handsome man? I wish I could
be impetuous and say what's on my mind,
but all rules militate against blatant truth.
It seems I have done the right thing for decades.
It has only made me a lonely man.

The waiter returns with food, places plates,
asks if there is anything else I need?
The ambiguity of the question pulls at my heart.
I swallow the answer, shake my head no.

As if this incident had happened on a chalkboard,
I will erase it from my mind as completely as I can.
I will go home, sit in a wingback chair, and wonder
why it is so impossible for me to share my humanity.

ASIAN

I'm getting a pedicure, try to ignore
the manicurist, a very young and boyish
Asian man. Flat chest, flat stomach suggest
he is this side of emaciation. He raises
an arm. T-shirt edges up to reveal
the beginning of a tattoo I suspect wraps
around his side and ends splayed across
his chest. He sees me glance at him
and looks away. We do this several times
within an hour.

He wears flip-flops, jeans, and an aristocratic
nonchalance. He speaks Vietnamese and English
fluently. He is efficient, an expert cutting, shaping,
painting, nails. His casual movements indicate
calm, cool, unconcerned.

The whole time I'm in the salon, I focus on him.
I want to know his mystery. We've never talked.
He must rise in the morning without combing
his naturally spiky hair.

I've never been attracted to an Asian before,
worry about developing a crush that can
only end with my ego's death. He is much
younger than I. Can I ask him to dinner?

Would he flinch and ridicule me? If I reach out,
will he jerk back thinking me old and freakish?

I slump from the salon without answers,
want to say something, even goodbye, but don't.

BENJAMIN

We have just met at a Fourth of July party.
I have listened to you pontificate about boxing
for over an hour. Your mind percolates idea
after idea, pompous but passionate.
You're thirty-one years old, plan to leave
for Las Vegas in three weeks where you hope
to make your professional mark.

Your body is thin as a lean strip of bacon.
When you bend, there is no sign of stomach.
I imagine without your shirt you are ripped.
You are an attractive young man in a rough
but clean-cut sort of way. Your dark brown
hair is cut short enough not to benefit
from a comb, but several times during our
conversation, you pull your hands over the top
of your head as if to make sure you're close-cropped.

Your green eyes probe mine as if asking why
I am spending so much time focused on you,
but still you continue to talk almost non-stop.
I smile a lot. It is my secret pleasure to give
myself a part of you.

When you leave, you don't acknowledge me
with goodbye or even a nod. You walk
into the night and disappear toward your car

parked out of sight . Whatever happened,
I regret if my face showed longing,
the ache I tried so hard to hide,
the ache I'm nearly dead from.

IN THE BANK LINE

A hinge on the door of desire squeaks
open on a man in hawk-black tennis shirt,
trousers, beard to match. He strides across
the parking lot. No one is allowed inside
because of Coronavirus, so this bank
worker approaches each car and asks
the driver what banking business is needed.
When he approaches my car, I roll down
the window, look up at his soft blue eyes,
his smile, white as clouds behind him.
He asks what I want to transact. I tell him
I want to withdraw some money. What
I really want to say sticks in my throat:
can we go for a coffee date? Can I
somehow wrangle a connection between us?
Will you come to my empty house, be my lover?
He hands me a paper on which I write
the amount I want to withdraw, then
he moves away from my window. I stare
after him, feel a pinch of panic because
I do not know what to do with this instant
attraction. I am the second car in a line of ten.
When it is my turn, I see his face in the video
monitor. Our exchange of common words
overrides everything I feel. Everything
I feel drives away with me like a ghost
on the passenger seat, dissolves into frustration
like a block of ice on a hot stove burner.

I drive through town toward home embracing
the warm nothingness my world comes to.
I would never have guessed the patience it takes
to recover from infatuation.

EVERYTHING ABOUT A NEWCOMER

You amble into the Al-Anon meeting,
a first-timer, workout-thin, ruddy complexion,
handsomest, youngest man in the room.
You slip into a chair at the far end of the table,
never remove your baseball cap. When you move,
sleeves of your tee-shirt ride upward,
reveal the beginning of tattoos. Your wedding
ring gleams from the glare of fluorescent light.

You catch me staring at you,
send back an uneasy look.
I work hard not to gawk,
resolve not to look at all.

Why should I reduce myself to begging
for a glance, for a signal that it is okay
to check you out. After all, you did not
come to this meeting to meet me.
You came with a tortured heart, troubled mind,
probably bereft of hope, and yet I want
to wrap my eyes around you.

All through the meeting I do not turn my head
in your direction again. You never speak.
You listen.

After the meeting, I give up timidity,
walk to you, extend my hand.
In a manner of greeting I embrace your skin,
tell you I look forward to seeing you next week.
I leave first, injured by infatuation.

V

MOMENTARY OCCURRENCES

*It's when you go out looking for
love that it costs you an arm & a
leg and it only lasts for one night.*

-Anthony T. Hincks

*Out stretched hands and
one night stands, still I can't
find love.*

-Kid Rock

CHECKING MYSELF OUT

At my aunt's sumptuous, Italian wedding
reception, I sat at a long table, laughing at things
that weren't funny, longing to be elsewhere.
Logically, I should have had a woman with me
to substantiate heterosexuality, even though
I suspected other men present were also
hiding secret lives behind the metaphorical drape.
I felt as if I needed to reproduce on the spot
to prove myself normal. The festivities stoked
my desire to drop into a gay bar for a bucketful
of Fireball Cinnamon Whiskey. A half hour later,
I provided appropriate goodbyes and left.

Unfamiliar with disreputable parts of Columbus,
I remembered someone once showing me
a streetcar-shaped bar in a back alley. I entered
to loud, disco music and a crowd of men high
on each other's conversation. A throng
of bodies packed the dance floor. I ordered
a Budweiser, wedged myself against the wall,
watched men flaunt their gayness as if it were
a religion. Out of nowhere a handsome blond
asked me to dance. I accepted. Lips close
to my ear, he invited me home on the condition
we give his roommate a ride.

I left with two strangers. Aware I'd had a death
wish all evening, I pictured myself in my coffin.
Within the hour, however, I discovered the blond
and his roommate were enrolled in master's degree
programs at The Ohio State University. Relief
flowed through me like an intoxicant.
I was not in the company of misfits. The roommate
went to bed. The blond and I lay sex aside, exchanged
life stories until two in the morning. He laughed
that I thought him a criminal who would do me harm.

I walked to my car on that balmy summer morning,
savoring the start of a friendship and the sensation of survival.

A THING PREDICTED

I followed to a dingy room in a downtown,
second-rate hotel. We lay naked on a single bed.
Cheap plastic curtains billowed with July breeze.
I had hung my clothes over an old-fashioned radiator.
"Take advantage of your youth now because
when you're older, no one will want you."
The message made sense, but I felt immune.
I was twenty-five and could not imagine
ever being old.

I lay on the bed with my arms behind my head,
thinking about those prophetic words. Had I been
told a secret, a special message from someone
who wanted to warn me not to take myself for granted?

Piece by piece I reached for my clothes, those words
etching themselves into my mind like a laser inscribes glass.

Fifty years later, truth of those words scream in my ears.
These nights, my clothes do not hang over a radiator
in a cheap hotel. They suspend neatly in the closet
as if I had a personal valet. I have a double bed,
designer curtains made from the finest cotton.
I sleep naked, unloved, and alone.

THIS SUNDAY

This Sunday, I'm taking a twenty-eight-year-old
to dinner. What do I say to someone so young?
Our conversation will be either a disposable
memory or a collectible souvenir. We will eat
in a restaurant that has the best Italian food
in Columbus. I will spread my cloth napkin
with extra precision. I will not mention
relationships that hollowed out my heart,
left me leery of love. Maybe we will talk
about literature, sports, jobs, pieces of himself
he wants to share. I hope the evening flows
like a blue river reflecting summer sky.

We first met in a bar's semi darkness,
I audaciously kissed his naked collarbone
after he'd finished dancing on a raised platform.
This time, I will memorize the shape of his face,
his luminous eyes. I will ask him to forgive me
for staring, my way of documenting someone
whom I hope will become more than a passerby.

The closer I get to this date, the more I anticipate
it. In fact, I have begun to live for the day
we will sit across from one another, water glasses
brought to our lips like unconscious kisses.

Thereafter, I will leave the next move to him,
to pull the last match from the matchbook of my life,
strike it against possibility or extinguish it
with one simple breath.

DINNER

It's a new beginning for both of us.
The waitress brings water we sip
while we make up minds what we want
to eat, how we will talk to each other
on this first date. Beneath light from pinup
lamps along the wall, we study each other's face,
compliment attire. You are much younger than I.

The waitress takes our order, Chicken Alfredo
for you, spaghetti for me, salads for both of us
with house dressing. Dimples accentuate your smile,
quick and bright. I see why you are
a popular stripper in the bar where I met you
last night.

Food arrives. You slip your fork into a mouthful
of noodles, but before you begin to eat,
announce that you are HIV. You pull a keychain
from your pocket, show me a very small metal
canister which holds the pill you take each day.

I want to ask how it feels to adjust
to a different way of living, but I don't.
I wonder if you are thinking my interest
in you has faded. I want to tell you
the bar has simply been raised, that
we can face the challenge together.

We go on eating. You grin a lot.
So do I. In less than an hour, you've
brought me very close to your truth.

After dinner, you walk to my car, hug me
as if you had found something of value
and lost it in the same day. I hug you back,
convinced I won't hear from you again,
and I don't.

SUNGLASSES

You never gave any indication
it was going to be no more than a hookup.
You left sunglasses on top of my bureau
which I assumed was a Freudian setup
to bring you back again. We exchanged
phone numbers, but I haven't heard
from you since you swaggered away.

I'm having a moment when nothing
has an explanation. Was there always
something hopeless about our meeting
that I didn't see because I was dazzled
by your dancer's body, instant thoughtfulness.
I've never felt loved so quickly, so thoroughly
by so few words.

At my house you kicked sandals aside,
slid from jeans, raised your shirt over your head
to reveal a well-defined chest. Light
from the hallway shadowed the room
and the brown glow of your Spanish body.

Afterwards, we listened to the silence
in the room, held each other as if to let go
we would fall from several stories high.

In the car, halfway to your house
you remembered your sunglasses
left atop the chest of drawers.
They're still there, untouched until I finally
accept it really was only a one night stand.

JUAN

It's Memorial Day, and I amble into a bar
for a drink I don't really want. A group
of four men sit to my left who have swallowed
feathers because their giggles are incessant.
I sit alone, a couple of seats away from them.
There are three vacant seats to my right.
After an hour and a half of gulping house
whiskey to keep loneliness under control,
a Latino man seats himself one stool away,
orders a Budweiser. He is magazine handsome,
occupied watching a dance program on his phone
with ear plugs hanging out of his head.

I'm usually not bold enough to buy someone
a drink, but after having had a few myself,
I feel otherworldly enough to risk rejection.
I signal the bartender to bring the stranger
another Budweiser. He accepts it graciously.

Soon, we are sharing personal histories.
Without warning he places his arm around
the back of my chair and goes on watching
the dance program. Finished, he removes
the earbuds, leans toward me, nuzzles my cheek
with the side of his face. His arm slides
around my shoulder and he squeezes.

We agree to walk to my car. As we drive,
his hand rests on my thigh. Gentle, gentle
touches, smooth and silent, that take
each and every shadow of solitude away.

TONY

You've been sipping "Sex on the Beach" all night,
becoming more and more irresponsible.
I have an impulse to ask you home, but, instead,
I just keep watching you get drunk. Your brown
eyes look at me as if you can take from me
whatever you want.

I buy you a drink, watch your body
in a sleeveless t-shirt, hard and dazzling
in semi dark. You exude indifference,
a pose that strips you of emotion,
of the insinuation of being too easy.
Do you have language beyond street slang?
I've strayed into your playground where
people astound my ears with camp, and
I listen to this blabbering crowd speak hours
of nothing.

You lean against the bar in a way that says
your flesh is for sale. I think you are dumb,
drunk, and uncaring about who waltzes you
out of here. I hover around the idea that
you are simply a gigolo, a user, someone
who strips once a week in this very bar,
comes back on nights off to trap unhappy
patrons in the palm of your hand, and yet
the stagnation of my own life triggers
an impulse to exchange phone numbers.

You tap yours into my phone, misspell
stripper, and hand the phone back to me.
We won't go home together, and
you'll never call me. I turn away,
head toward my car, think
not everything is about lust

YOU COME MY WAY, AND I THINK YOU'RE WICKED

Imagine me in mid-afternoon
lying on the loveseat in my boxers
with an intention to nap when the sound
of your incoming text message draws
my attention to the cell phone screen.
There's been nothing between us,
a few hours in a bar, inane chitchat,
a few glasses of "Sex on the Beach."
You did, however, smooth talk me
into exchanging phone numbers.
You ask me how I am and follow that
with a request for money, saying
you will pay me back next week.
I ignore the request, accuse you
of seeing me as an easy mark.
You assure me you are not like that.
When I ask you what kind of work
you do, you say you flap houses
which means you hang drywall. I also
learn you have had your driver's
license suspended twice for drunk
driving and that you have a parole
officer. In other words, you are bad
news. Like Capote and Williams,
I'm lost when it comes to resisting
bad news.

The texting ends with your suggestion
we meet at the bar on Wednesday.
My curiosity could lead me into the hands
of a out-and-out user who would like
nothing more than to empty my pockets.
I need to sidestep this one, put an end
to incipient lust.

YOU SHOULD HAVE COME TO ME

I collapse into a white wicker chair
on the front porch after a day of despair,
of burning gasoline to run errands.
I thought I could do it all in one day: graduation
cards, groceries, getting together with a neighbor
for lunch. Meanwhile, day gathers the fire
of dusk in a dogwood tree, and I ring
my hands waiting to hear from you.

Considering the look of laughter in your eyes
the night we met, I was your Gigolo's joke,
the first of the evening to be amazed by your
illiterate street talk, the first of the evening to feed
you drink after drink and dare to think I mattered.

Tinnitus in my head grows louder, the sound
of crickets, not real. I look out over the lawn
that costs $78 a month to keep as green as
the felt on a billiard table.

When I saw you walk through the door of the bar,
I allowed myself to capture your attention,
a part-time stripper, probably a school dropout.
You sidled up, looked sidelong at me. We sat
shoulder-to-shoulder. An exchange of few words
lead to a conversation strung with cliches
like an inane verbal necklace. I wanted to ask

you to stop my loneliness. Instead we exchanged
phone numbers without any promises.

Dusk is darker now, and everything a silhouette.
I wait as the hours pile up and come to nothing.

EXPLAINING YOUR BODY

I glide hands over coveted skin.
You lie on sheets damp with desire.
I feel your sharp intake of breath.
Do I caress you too much, sinking
thumbs into the tenderest part
of your muscled back? You have
not spoken since my fingers began
sampling you. Now, you tremble
like an erotic bed trembles
when the heart, numbed by ecstasy,
succumbs to soft whispers.
I trace your jawbone, ribs, calves,
kiss your neck, all surfaces I find
in semi-dark. So it is that I fulfill
you with all I have to offer.

Later, you reach for cigarettes,
burning orange tip a poor man's
candlelight. In seconds we button
our lives back up, stuff our hearts
into a back pocket. What madness
made us think we should hunger
for more?

EXCEPTIONAL BREAKFAST

I awaken beside you with carnal burning,
greet you with words that tell how,
as we slept, January ice created stars
on the window. At the breakfast table,
I say I love you until I can hardly breathe.

The room is a small place called kitchen,
a name for where we peel down our needs
and circle each other with temporary arms.

Last night, my mind went wild with prayer
to keep us together forever. I look across
at you and touch your hand, soft as new grass.

Have I ruined us with too much
open talk about desire? I kiss your wrist,
hungry for a great silence in the kitchen,
so we can speak to that mysterious God,
ask not to be hurt being each other's lover,
ask that when we reach out for water,
it not turn to tears.

LATE DATE

The door opens, and you enter
at half past midnight, order Jack and Coke
which mirrors what I'm drinking. Semisonic's
"Closing Time" floods out conversation.
You settle on a stool beside me. We lean
toward each other's ear, utter loud introductions.

On the dance floor, the crowd reaches
toward ceiling as if to grasp rhythms to match
gyrating hips. Foreheads sweat. Eyes roll back
from one intoxicant or another.

Your skin glows from colored globes placed
intermittently around the bar.   We talk briefly,
intimacy, immediate, accentuated by leaning
closer every time we speak. I long
for something to happen, to become
the object of someone's instant caring.
Your dark eyes focus on mine. You ask
what I'm thinking. I answer, "About you."

Undistracted by surroundings, our eyes
continue to meet. I swallow diffidence,
ask you to dance to Enrique Inglesias
"Hero." Arms around each other,
our feet barely lift from the floor.

It seems the only thing that matters is
being held. We drift and drift beyond
the edges of music. "Come to my house,"
you say, and I nod yes, impatient to give
touches I've stored for countless years.

SUDDEN DESTINY

In white g-string you have just finished
dancing on a platform under colored lights,
begun to work the crowd around the bar.
You know how to rub against other people's
fantasies to collect dollars in your waistband.

When you come to me, your whole demeanor
changes. You slowly put your arms around me.
I rest my face in the crook of your neck,
inhale sweet cologne. I sense
this is not part of your practiced act,
but something you want. In an audacious move,
I kiss your collarbone. You do not pull away
or change position. We seem to talk about
everything in a few minutes. I learn your name,
your job, a hint of the heartbreaks that killed
your previous relationships. We hug again.
Your nearly-naked body breathes against mine,
and I kiss your neck once more. You do not hesitate
to keep your arms around me. Before you leave
for another dance gig in yet another bar,
you return to me four times as if to tell me
you have not forgotten the serendipity
of our connection.

Our last embrace finds our lips nearly touching.
Before you leave, you tap your number

into my phone, and we agree to have dinner
together soon. You leave and, although barely
knowing you, I feel bereft.

Afterwards, I question why you chose me
from among others, especially at my age?
I imagine you will become reasonable and not call.
I will, though, be waiting, telling hope not to soar
to quickly in a world where people constantly turn
away from love.

H.C.

His bedroom is littered with broken dreams,
stacks of dirty laundry he stands ankle-deep in.

Down in the basement, he has rigged
a massage parlor, promises a healthy rub
down and a happy ending. Reared
in Southern Ohio poverty, he wants
to prove a success by placing hands
upon immodest needs of mostly married men.
A meager tax-free income of forty dollars
per client doesn't cancel destitution.

He smokes dollar-a-pack cigarettes,
lies about how his rich husband bought him
a car he can't afford to drive.

He does not squander middle age on hope,
buried during twenty years of caregiving
for five family members.

His modus operandi disincludes romantic
commitment. Aside from an occasional
hookup on the internet, he walks the earth
alone and makes love to what he can
easily let go of.

A PAGE OF PASSION FROM THE BOOK OF BLUE

You offer your hand to help me up
to the top of an extra high bed
quilted with layers of softness. You
pull me against velvet, brown skin
and parallel warmth.

The weir of a ceiling fan mingles
with monotony of an interview show.
We lull within safe silence
of each other's arms, stillness against
stillness. We sink into a place where
absence of words is better
than language. Under the blankets,
knees and fingers burn for closer contact.
Our legs tangle in an unmoving dance.
We are not young. Our bones tell truths,
but we have given younger selves
to each other tonight.

When I slip out of bed, you guide me
down, a steady hand on my upper arm
until my feet touch hardwood. I find
my clothes in a pile, balance into them,
and there you are, holding me
from all sides, encircling me
with the pulse of your heart atop mine.

VI

IN A LAND OF STONES

Somebody, your father or mine, should have told us that not many people have ever died of love. But multitudes have perished, and are perishing every hour- and in the oddest places!-for the lack of it.

-James Baldwin

Why is it that, as a culture, we are more comfortable seeing two men holding guns than holding hands?

-Ernest Gaines

DEPICTING THE SORROW OF BEING A
CHILDHOOD QUEER

Peers called me names when I was young,
language that kept friends and buddies on the fringe.
When those words hit me, I would ask why?
Was it because I was Italian? Each morning,
like a homeless child, I awoke feeling alienated
from family. Breathing the same air, but a part
of them only through conformity.

I counted hours before they would discover
a secret even I didn't understand. It was as if
God had planted an explosive under my belt
without me knowing it. At eight years old,
I suspected the wrong word or wrong move
would detonate me.

I kept so stoic a face on the bus
that took me to St Joseph's camp
that summer, I appeared dead.
I tried to make myself vanish
from the seat opposite a conspicuous bully.
He badgered me with taunts, tried to get me
to move or speak in ways different
from himself. I walled him off with
weak bravado, stared him in the eyes
with counterfeit confidence. He wasn't fooled.
I was, in thinking I had hidden
the center of myself from him.

No dad had ever taught me to slug
against derogatory accusations.
I failed again and again to make a fist.
I had no defense except invisibility.

That's the story of how I walked the earth,
scavenged for shelter, learned magic
of disappearing from the truth inside me.

STRAIGHTENING UP

I was told as a kid to swing my arms
when I walked, or people would think
I was queer. That piece of advice killed me,
turned me into a ghost of myself.
So in high school halls or on streets of Columbus,
I swung my arms vigorously, at the ends
of which were clenched fists.

Eventually, out of the fog of sexual identification,
I learned to disregard damaging good
intentions of others, but for years, I wouldn't
look in the eyes of anyone coming toward me,
fearful I would be categorized
and condemned. Sporadically, I allowed
my body to behave naturally, but, most of the time,
I attempted to satisfy everyone around me.

I was not flagrantly classifiable, but do-gooders
made me feel that I was one wrong step away
from being burnt at the social stake. I lived
through a prejudiced and unaccepting period
of history, a time when McCarthyism underscored
already existent narrow-mindedness. Paranoia
caused people to slam doors shut on tolerance,
acceptance, and common sense.

Even today, when I walk into a straight bar,
I feel as if my masculinity is being questioned,
as if eyes of patrons are ready to classify me.
Little do they suspect that my closet has room
for some of them.

A CROOKED CHILDHOOD

I have an obsession with the seedy
side of life. Being born in the South End
of Columbus, spending formative years there
accounts for preoccupation with the sordid
and unsavory.

On the other hand, when I lived in the South End,
it was a multicultural ideal, free of gangs,
constant crime. Yet, even as a boy, I sensed
underlying rot of humanity that could surface
at any moment. And it did, years later,
after I'd moved to the suburbs.

In the 40s and 50s, it was safe to walk streets
and alleys. I identified with the less fortunate.
I gained insight into other people's harder ways.
I mingled without feeling superior.

Truth be told, I've always had a fascination
with the disreputable side of life. Maybe it was
because my dad sold beer on Sunday when
the blue laws were in place, wrote numbers,
bribed local police, and accidentally left
a 16 mm pornographic film on my toy projector.

I learned about different liquors in our confectionery,
watched alcoholics sway down streets after my dad
fortified them with a pint of wine on credit.

I was a little boy who learned too much too soon
about the unwholesome side of life. I was slightly
ashamed of what I knew and carried guilt for knowing it.

THE MINGLING OF BLOOD

Sun burns golden as the statue of Ares
and Aphrodite in sky the color of dad's
baby blue necktie. Spring glimmers
as if everything we're made of green,
delicate glass, blossoms, white as past snows.

I'm sitting on the porch, listening to peeper's
high-pitched call, thinking how it feels
to be an old man in a young season.
My eyes burn a little thinking about a friend
I lost one spring when we were both eighteen.

Jim dropped out of college the first quarter
of his freshman year and joined the paratroopers.
Part of a brigade on maneuvers over Wilmington,
Ohio, he was prepared to parachute when
the plane crashed. The funeral was pomp
and military circumstance, as greatly attended
as a burial for a hero killed at war.

On yet a different spring day, we sat on a log
by Alum Creek. Each of us delicately swept
a blade across our ular artery, pressed our wrists
together, and swore brotherhood forever.

I still carry a photo of him sitting on back porch steps
at his house on Woodrow Avenue when he was a junior
in high school. It was a beautiful spring moment that day too.

139

I've carried that photo in my wallet since 1964.
He was the kind of kid who walked down the halls
at school, and everyone knew his name. I think of him
often. Particularly on a spring day like today,
I resurrect his memory and stare at my wrist.

UNION STATION IS REAL

Sun has smothered twilight, suffocated night
with unbearable humidity. Sandy and I saunter
along High Street on the Ohio State University
campus, looking for an open business that sells
food and drink. After walking several blocks,
feeling defeated, I suggest Union Station.

We slide into the car, head south toward Short North,
a trendy upscale section of Columbus. Again we park
blocks away, begin the long trek to our destination.

We arrive, climb a cement ramp to the entrance,
greeted by a young man whose extravagant
hand gestures are reminiscent of a flock of birds
taking off in various directions at the same time.
His high-pitched, nasal affability leads to our table.
The waiter, boyish, with partially bleached brown hair,
wears shorts so tight and skimpy denim disappears
on his backside until I believe I can hear his butt
yammering for help. He takes our order for two
margaritas, veggie pizza, and minces away, tattoos
on his calves marking his exit.

The place is packed with mostly men singing along
to neverending show tunes. Sandy and I scream
at each other to be heard. It would be impossible
to detect a lion's roar amidst the unrestrained
pandemonium.

Our waiter returns, flutters drinks and pizza onto the table,
flies away, feet barely touching the ground.

We finish eating, pay the bill, leave this temporary world
held together by an overflow of fun
and an outpouring of social solidarity.

WHO WOULD HAVE KNOWN?

I ripped my leg hurtling a chain-link fence.
Blood, red as the center of a Japanese flag,
rolled to my ankle. I ignored the tear, happy
to be on the other side of the "Closed" sign
fastened to the gate of Millbrook Apartments'
private swimming pool.

Humidity, like a wool blanket, smothered
July night. My cousin, Butch, and
our friend, Jim, followed me over the fence.
Chlorine had never been so inviting.
We were drunk on determination
to cool our bodies. Moonlight spread
sparkles over water as we slipped beneath it,
the only sound as we rose to the surface, water
breaking from our bodies like liquid glass.

I was also drunk on my nearness to Jim,
a handsome high school junior who would
join paratroopers after graduation and die
that year when his practice plane malfunctioned
during maneuvers over Wellington, Ohio.
We had sliced our wrists the summer before,
became blood brothers. This night, however,
was about risk and carefree frolic before
servicemen would place a flag over Jim's coffin
in less than two years. Every girl wanted him,
but he confessed one night to wanting me.

I ignored him, changed the topic, and we never spoke
of it again. A few months passed, and
he became engaged to Susan Moore.

Fifty years later, I still wonder if I had given in,
would that have prevented him from proving
himself more of a man by falling from the sky?

SELF PORTRAIT

Sixty years later, I finally understand
how much I wounded you.

We sat on a log by Alum Creek.
July sun hung in the sky like a sharp
knife causing severe burn to exposed skin.
In the shade, our shadows lay before us
black as disappointment. You asked me
if I had ever wanted to do something more
than anything else in the world?

Until that moment, our conversation had been
small talk with long stretches of silence.
Greenish-brown creek water rippled past,
echoed into the stand of trees behind us.
I could smell Sweet-After-Death and Wild
Ginger. I could smell my own nervous sweat.
You were twenty-seven. I was seventeen.
It was 1958, a time before the underside
of everything went public, a time when
insight into myself was still innocent. Yet,
in some non-verbal way I sensed
what you wanted, and then you said it.
"I want to kiss you."

My stomach felt as if I'd swallowed snow.
I worried I'd embarrass either of us

by what I did or did not say. A few
minutes passed. I asked you to take me home.
We said nothing else.

I slumped into the bathroom,
felt weak as dust, guilty of something
unnameable, studied myself in the mirror.
The face was the same thin face, and though
I didn't have a portrait of myself hidden
in the attic like Dorian Gray, I thought
if I looked long enough, I'd find moral decay,
a hint of depravity because I had become
the object of male admiration.

SOLEMNLY ALONE IN THE STREET

At age eight, my parents have left me
asleep, trusting I will be okay this once
without a babysitter, but I awaken, calm
at first, then fearful. Brain pumping fear
of my own freedom, I stuff myself into
clothes, flee the house, start down
6th Street toward my parents' confectionery.
I don't really know my way.
I stand beneath streetlight,
peering at birdless, black sky, stars
a terrible distance away, wonder how
I can think about my thinking. Traffic
does not devour roads in 1949. I dwell
in the intersection of Hinman and 6th Street
for a long time without worry. Then,
I begin to roam down the middle
of asphalt, counting blocks. After eight,
I know I am either lost or very near
my destination. I turn the corner onto Barthman
Avenue, hear the buzz of neon, see light
from confectionery windows. Inside,
a line of customers preoccupy my parents
who are so busy they barely recognize
I have broken the rules. They leave me alone
until closing time when I unravel my story.
I try to explain about my epiphany
beneath the streetlight. I escape punishment

in lieu of a lecture. For a few moments,
I am their little desperado who gets off easy,
who in his heart knows full well
God disapproves of desperados.

LIBRARY THIEF

I used to steal books from the library.
My conscience was in abeyance
during that time. I would climb marble
stairways to the second floor, enter a room
marked "Arts" where shelves of poetry books
were kept. Each trip, I slipped one or two
under sweatshirt or coat, feeling guilt
exonerated by the fact that the books
were poetry. I don't know how my mind
twisted it so it was not okay to steal
other books, but it was okay to steal poetry.

Even so, I walked with a soft shoe
past the lady at the desk with whom
I had established a very warm and cordial
acquaintanceship, prerequisite to thievery.
I think she knew every time I absconded,
but she liked me enough not to investigate
beyond a penetrating stare in my direction.
She was short, frumpy, middle-aged
with a pretty face and the compassion
to allow me to steal the only thing that
mattered to me at the time.

Eventually, my shenanigans turned
into a game. She knew, and I knew she knew,
and she knew that I knew she knew.

Each trip down marble steps was not guiltless.
I hunched up, found my way to the door,
expecting security to snatch me
by the neck and imprison me for life.
I felt certain as I passed the guard my face told
on me. I may as well have been wearing a cowbell
around my neck with the word guilty painted in red.
With books safe in the trunk, myself in the car,
I held my breath until I left the parking lot,
having bartered innocence for a few books of poetry.

NOWHERE WAS I MORE LONELY THAN AT THE PRIDE PARADE

My hair cutter had client parking
behind her salon, invited me to accompany
her to the parade. I'd never been before,
thought I should take advantage of this
invitation because parking in the vicinity
is a problem.

I was prepared for any version
of Mardi Gras esque celebration,
but I was unprepared for ubiquitous
camaraderie that spread throughout
the crowds like a delicious rumor.
I felt pent-up energy of those bursting
to be free of pretense, to step into
a more comfortable identity.

I've often wondered what it would feel like,
look like for people to put aside self-deception
and posturing. This occasion insisted a person
drop everyday masks. Of course, there were
extremes: Adonises with sculpted bodies
barely clad in loincloths, drag queens
whose gowns could not possibly hold
one more sequin. Their wigs made
Dolly Parton look bald.

Same-sex couples held hands without threat,
didn't hesitate to kiss. Whitman would have
been proud of these hours of honesty.
Aside from my hair cutter, I had no special person
with whom to share my deepest feelings,
so I followed her through the crowd, all the time
aware of a vacancy beside me that even an
unconventional, unconditional celebration couldn't fill.

BOXES

When I was sixteen, I held a part-time job
at a flower shop in the Hartman building
downtown. A hillbilly boy, about my age,
and I mostly worked folding boxes
in a storage room in the basement.
He had greasy hair, pimply face, wrinkled
clothes.

We sat on a concrete floor, surrounded
by stacks of boxes with bend marks
showing us where to fold. He liked to talk
dirty about his girlfriend and their sex life.
I didn't know how much of it was wishful
thinking or truth.   He bullied me to talk
about my girlfriend and our sex life.
The latter did not exist in the 1950s,
but to save myself, I invented both.

I wanted to kick him out and be alone,
or quit my job and go home. He seemed
desperate to prove me less a man than he,
insinuated I was queer, and I felt unsafe
alone in the basement with him.
He tyrannized and tormented. Sometimes,
I felt as if I were working with an attack dog.
In the flower business, some seasons are better
than others, and when the number of orders
slacked off, I lost my job.

I walked down State Street and around the corner
to 3rd, caught the bus home, pumped to be rid
of a thug-like persecutor and my need to pretend.

VII

A MISCELLANEOUS RIFF

The broken guitar strings,
this silence deafening.
His voice,
missing.

-Mansi Agarwala

HIDDEN GUITAR

I've hidden a guitar in the closet
between an old suitcase and two rifles
leaning against the back wall. I bought it
for $37.99 at Lev's Pawn Shop.
It's the color of a hard-blue January sky.

I don't know how to play one note.
I've never taken lessons. I just like
having it. Sometimes, I get teary-eyed
listening to guitar music, particularly
somber chords. A few times I've dragged
the guitar from the closet late at night,
strummed it like a waking weakness
to hug something to myself.

I love to sit in the dining room window
in the winter when it's snowing,
attempt to pick out a tune, vibration
of each string an amateurish incompetence
bumbling fingers fret.

Truth is, maybe I don't want to learn guitar.
Maybe joy comes from holding it close
to my chest where my dad once tied me
in a kitchen chair.

I don't want self-teaching books
or instruction from an expert.
I am the expert, the kid who once hid
in the closet because, at the time,
it seemed the safest place to be.

R. Nikolas Macioci earned a PhD from The Ohio State University, and for thirty years taught for the Columbus City Schools. In addition to English, he taught Drama and developed a Writers Seminar for select students. OCTELA, the Ohio Council of Teachers of English, named Nik Macioci the best secondary English teacher in the state of Ohio. Nik is the author of eleven books. *Cafes of Childhood* (the original chatbook with additional poems), critics and judges called a "beautifully harrowing account of child abuse," but not "sentimental" or "self-pitying," an "amazing book," and "a single unified whole." *Cafes of Childhood* was submitted for the Pulitzer Prize in 1992. In 2020, he was nominated for a Pushcart Prize. In addition, more than two hundred of his poems have been published here and abroad in magazines and journals, including *The Society of Classical Poets Journal, Chiron, Concho River Review, The Bombay Review, Tipton Poetry Journal,* and *Blue Unicorn.*

He won First Place in the 1987 National Writer's Union Poetry Competition, judged by Denise Levertov, First Place in The Baudelaire Award Competition, sponsored by The World Order of Narrative and Formalist Poets (1989), Second Place in Zone 3's first annual Rainmaker Awards, judged by Howard Nemerov (1989), and Second Place in the Writer's Digest annual competition, judged by Diane Wakoski (1991).

www.ingramcontent.com/pod-product-compliance
Lightning Source LLC
Chambersburg PA
CBHW030328100526
44592CB00010B/615